ORIGINAL PIANOFORTE PIE

BOOK II
(Grades 1 & 2)

THE ASSOCIATED BOARD OF THE ROYAL SCHOOLS OF MUSIC

Haymaker's Dance

FELIX SWINSTEAD

Allegretto grazioso

All Forlorn

WILLIAM ALWYN

The Lonely Cottage

IVOR R. FOSTER

At Sundown

THOMAS F. DUNHILL

Over the Border

JESSIE FURZE

Neat and steady

Minuet in G

DOROTHY PILLING

Summer Rain

LAVENA WOOD

Valse-Lullaby

NORMAN ASKEW

poco a poco a tempo al tempo I

Study in F

GEORGE DYSON

A Sea Song

C. H. STUART DUNCAN

Cello Solo

C. S. LANG

Andante maestoso

p

cantabile e ben marcato

mf *p*

cresc.

f *mf* *poco rall.* *p*

The Desolate Farmhouse

THOMAS A. JOHNSON

Lullaby for a Chinese Infant

GORDON JACOB

Marching Song

KENNETH V. JONES

April Dance

ALAN RICHARDSON

A Study in Time

ROY TEED

Tristesse

TERENCE GREAVES

The Shepherd Plays his Pipe

DAVID BRANSON

Waltz

STUART THYNE

A Little Pastoral

(from an old manuscript)

ANGUS MORRISON

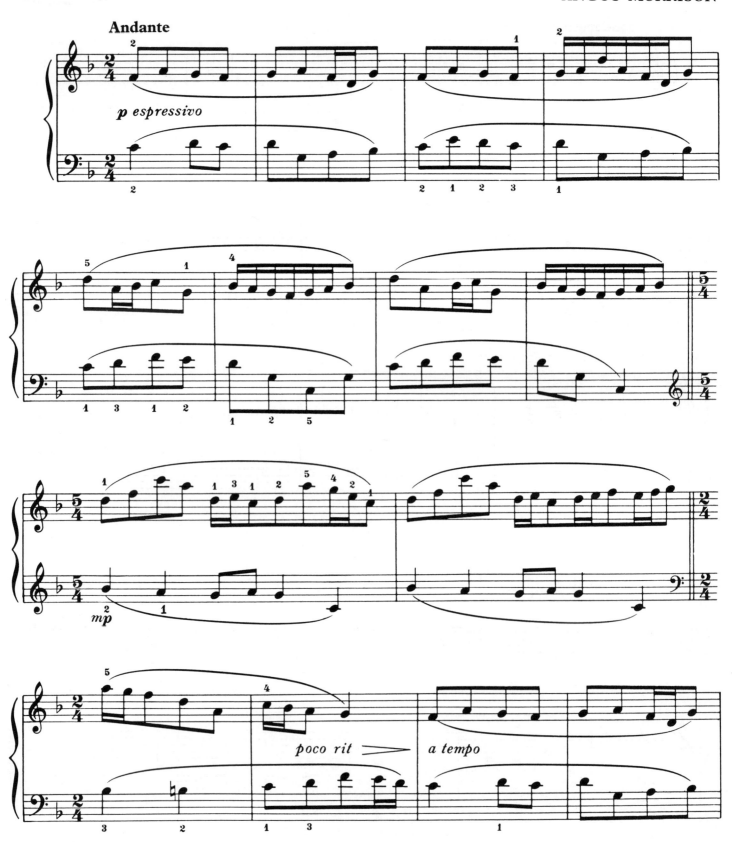

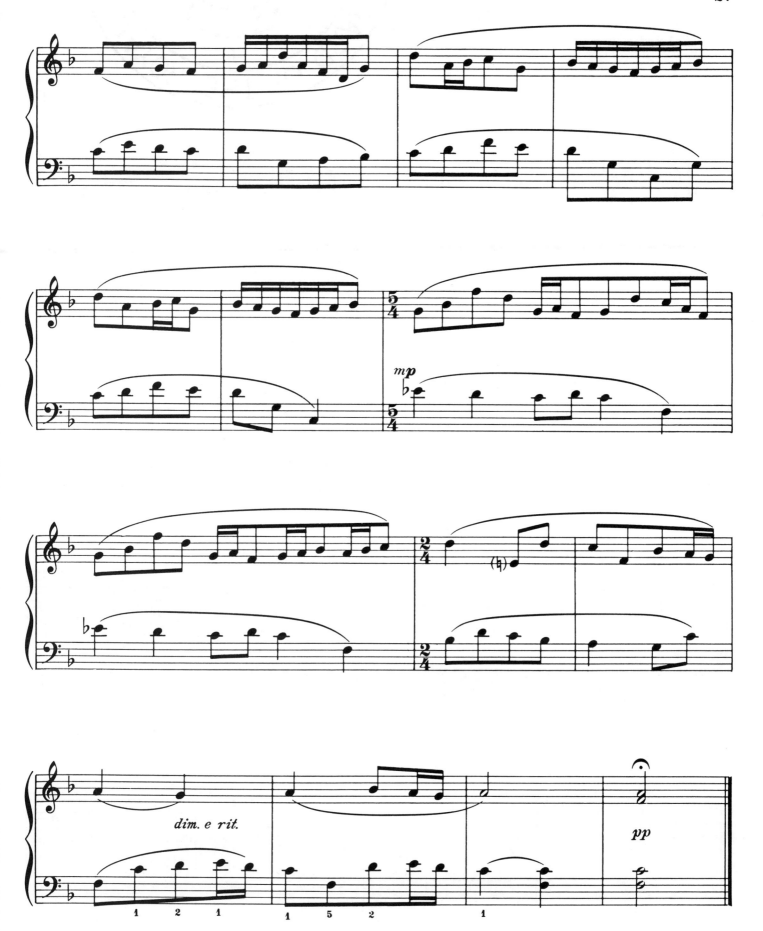

Little Habañera

JEAN MACKIE

Saying Goodbye

TIMOTHY BAXTER

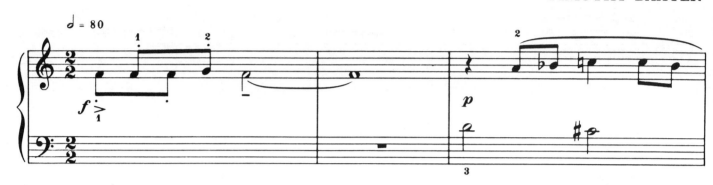

Festivity

HAROLD R. CLARK

Allegro e sempre ben ritmico

AB 1729

Printed in England by Caligraving Limited Thetford Norfolk

2:01